Strategic Planning for Action and Results

Edited by Lindsay Geddes

Contents

From the President

Achieving corporate goals in the 1990s presents challenges that call for outstanding planning—and outstanding execution. External factors such as increasingly sophisticated customers and competitors, and internal considerations such as changing employee expectations make it imperative for companies to manage strategically.

Today's strategic management integrates planning with management systems that encourage action to attain corporate goals. What used to be separate activities and functional specialties are being joined. Strategic planning and human resources together support the efforts of both line executives and employees to serve customers, build competitive advantage, generate the best possible financial results and create value for shareholders.

The highlights from the Strategic Management Conference presented here contain insights and information about theories and practices that work for leading companies.

I would like to thank the speakers at the conference for sharing their views and experiences and the attendees for their active participation and perceptive questions.

PRESTON TOWNLEY
President and CEO

Executive Summary

The Conference Board's 13th Annual Strategic Management Conference was held for the first time in two locations, New York and Los Angeles. Audiences heard about the latest and best theories and practices in strategic management at both corporate and operating levels.

Competitive and economic pressures continue to drive the trend toward simplicity. Elaborate systems of the past produced lengthy documentation making implementation a problem. Today's streamlined approach starts with line executives' preparation of short, simple paperwork used for discussion and agreement on direction and action.

The emphasis on implementation is focusing attention on human issues. The "soft" side of management—culture, communication, trust and training—is as important as the "hard" side—restructuring, investments, productivity improvement and cost reduction. The role of human resources is growing accordingly. But the behavior of executives and managers at all levels is the force behind change and the team is the key mechanism for action.

Companies are therefore working on minimizing internal barriers and increasing coordination. The audience heard how:

- *Becton Dickinson* reduces management layers and relies on teams of people from different geographic areas, business units and functions to coordinate strategy and management systems;

- *Siemens* coordinates value-adding activities globally and *Nissan* achieves effective communication between disparate cultures;

- *Bristol-Myers Squibb's* planning efforts unify R&D, marketing and manufacturing activities; at *Union Camp*, strategic planning and human resources work together at all levels; and

- *Northwestern Memorial Hospital* integrates strategy and the human resource system to remove barriers to action.

In addition, as they seek to exploit overseas opportunities and optimize resources, companies are giving employees support and direction and delegating responsibility for results. Speakers described how:

- *GE's* Work-Out Program is refocusing the work force's efforts to help deliver value to customers;

- at *IBM* and *Outboard Marine* the key to operating successfully overseas is appointing local managers;

- *AT&T's* efforts based on corporate strengths increase competitive advantage and earnings growth; and

- at *National Medical Enterprises, Allied-Signal* and *Avery Dennison*, the CEO's involvement in setting direction ripples through the entire organization.

Planning has evolved from a "sometime thing" to an activity that directly affects a company's prospects. Strategic management is crucial in helping a company achieve its long-term goals while meeting short-term challenges.

Managing Strategically— Nothing Less Will Do!

Walter B. Schaffir

President, Growth Dynamics, Inc.

Conference Chairman

A while back, *The Wall Street Journal* carried a story on Seamier Cray, who later founded Cray Research. Cray was once asked to produce a one-year plan and a five-year plan. The next day, he produced two binders. Each contained a single sheet of paper. In the first binder, Cray had written: "Five-Year Plan—to produce the world's fastest computers." The sheet in the second binder read: "One-Year Plan—to complete one-fifth of the five-year plan." The days of taking strategic planning lightly are probably gone forever.

Every line manager in all but the most casually run company knows that a strategic plan is no longer an option: It is expected. Yet planning in many companies has become overly bureaucratic. Our preoccupation with systems, paperwork and fads has given strategic planning a bad name. Too many of us still have to shift from complying with dogmatic planning systems to thinking strategically. This means thinking in terms of how opportunities, threats, strengths and weaknesses offer choices and how direction shapes competitive advantage.

In our eagerness to develop a document, we forget that the purpose of planning is not to develop a plan! Rather, it is to get something done—to bring about some change. The planning document is merely the vehicle to get us there.

It is managing strategically—not merely developing a plan—that is the name of the game. This means managing on a day-to-day basis within the framework of an explicit, agreed-upon strategy. Managing strategically is a line operating responsibility. Staff can play a crucial role, but determining strategy is not a staff job.

No Single Best Way

I'm often asked, "Who is doing some really outstanding strategic planning?" and find myself hard-pressed for an answer. I usually say, "A few companies do an outstanding job most of the time," or "Most companies have good strategy some of the time," or "All companies do a lousy job at one time or another." My point is, good strategy is rare and success is short-lived.

Consider the succession of management doctrines served up in recent years. No sooner did we accept as gospel Peters' and Waterman's "Search For Excellence" than a *Business Week* article pointed out that most of the corporations Peters and Waterman cited no longer merit "excellence" ratings. No sooner did we master what seemed an orderly method of strategic analysis than we learned that what's really needed is "creative chaos" (which made us feel right at home). No sooner did Michael Porter dazzle us with his "value chain," promising competitive advantages in "two flavors"—low cost or differentiation—than Rosabeth Kantor argued that real competitive advantage arises from people and more flexible organizational arrangements. And the portfolio matrix, once the centerpiece of any respectable strategic plan, is rarely used these days.

In the course of this puzzling evolution, we began to understand that what appears to be conflict may in fact work to our advantage. For example, planned and "opportunistic" strategies don't necessarily conflict. A new opportunity may be outside the plan, but it surfaced because a plan was developed. Similarly, tension and consensus don't necessarily conflict. Stanford Pascale urges "constructive contention." Organizations thrive on tension at least in developing strategy; but we need teamwork and consensus to execute strategy.

Change Agents, Too, Must Keep Changing

And now, when we thought it was finally safe to roll out brave new programs to effect cultural change,

Michael Beer of Harvard warns us against the "fallacy of programmatic change." Lasting change, says Beer, cannot be brought about by large-scale programs, even when endorsed at the top. Rather, he says, the best way to effect change is through task-aligned teams that cross organization lines and work towards concrete goals. The point is, one can't change people by preaching to them, but one can change their behavior by having them work toward mutually agreed-upon objectives.

Whether line managers, staff or outside consultants, we are in danger of becoming entrenched in too much doctrine. We must all be open to change, but avoid being taken in by fads. The purpose of this and future conferences is to help us make sense of various planning approaches and the perplexing issues that surround them.

Leading the Way to Strategic Action

Roy H. Ekrom
President and Chief Executive Officer
Allied-Signal Aerospace Company

For me, strategic management starts with the belief that people want to do a good job and live up to their leader's expectations. So it follows that you, the leader, must think and manage strategically if your organization is going to do so.

The leader, of course, is ultimately responsible. You must have a vision of where you want the organization to go and of the strategies that will take it there. While other people may help shape the vision and strategies, you must be seen to be most fully committed to them. The vision and strategies must be easily understood, the products of clear thinking. They must be compatible with the organization's basic values as well as ethical and timely. And they must address fundamental business issues and embody expectations of greatness.

The Strategic Leader's Role

I think an important element of the strategic leader's role resembles that of the storyteller of old who by recounting past glories and heroic accomplishments encouraged a new generation to adopt the vision and to believe in their ability to achieve. Similarly, I think the key to effective implementation of strategy is encouraging people to believe in the strategy and in the value of their successfully implementing it. Indeed, the need to externally monitor implementation decreases when people throughout the organization have internalized the vision and can assign the right priorities for themselves.

Several years ago, I was asked to take over a troubled company. We decided to fix it rather than close it. Scaling back the company substantially exacerbated people's loss of faith and acceptance of failure. So we had to create a picture—a visualization—of success. We did this by resurrecting images of the wonderful man who had founded the company and of its past glory. We gave speeches to anyone who would listen—

at lunchtime bridge games, to people waiting for their car pool, anywhere. Slowly, we were able to turn the tide until almost everyone came to believe in the possibility of restoring the company to its historical prominence. Building belief in that vision was an arduous task, but it brought us to where we could begin creating and implementing strategic thinking.

More recently, I was asked to bring together two successful organizations with remarkably different cultures. To unify and integrate them, we again reached for the power of a rallying vision.

We had to learn to work together because the two organizations' products and systems are synergistic. We had thought that communicating a vision of combined greatness would transfer allegiance from separate heritages. We found that wasn't enough to get people to work together.

To build two-way trust and respect, my wife and I invited our division presidents, key staff people, and their spouses to spend a few days in a resort-like setting. During recreation and social time, we got to know each other. As everyone became acquainted, couples began to talk. Slowly, employees discovered that they shared many values and that they could work well together. The benefits of this social interaction were soon evident as people accepted what they'd resisted before. Our division managers now think almost immediately of combining their efforts to the company's advantage.

Managing strategically at the company level is one thing; doing so within each division is another. Only some of our 27 division managements felt comfortable thinking beyond day-to-day operations and dealing with the concepts of vision and strategy. Our challenge was to ensure that everyone learned to feel comfortable. To make vision and strategy real, rather than esoteric, we talked about them in any forum we could find. We explained the need to have a vision and to create plans and to undertake action to move toward it. Our division strategy review sessions now emphasize a discussion of strategic vision and what's being done to move towards it. We hardly discuss financial performance or short-term accomplishment in that forum at all.

Getting to know each other, learning to trust and work together, and making vision and strategy real have paid off. Today we are the third largest aerospace supplier in the world, and are firmly on the path to greatness.

Leadership, Not Trappings

Ultimately, effecting change is what strategic management and leadership are all about. Yet it's easy to mistake trappings for substance. Our continuing concern is that a division may adopt planning buzzwords and the latest strategic management programs without a real commitment to change. It is easy to be in constant motion without making real progress. Only when a division's management accepts and acts on the basic need to change will it realize improvements.

In the end it is up to strategic leaders and managers to communicate the need and desire to change and to provide the resources to make it happen. At our company, using the simple but powerful ideas discussed here has been and will continue to be the key to successful strategic management of change.

Using Strategic Planning To Lead the Corporation

Charles D. Miller
Chairman and Chief Executive Officer
Avery Dennison Corporation

Six months ago, Avery merged with Dennison Manufacturing Company. Our combined 1990 sales were about $2.6 billion. Our core businesses are office products, pressure-sensitive adhesives and materials, and product identification and control systems used principally in durable goods, health care and retailing.

When I joined Avery as the corporate planning director, I set out to push planning responsibility down to profit center management and to inject a sense of urgency. Now the real planners are the division general managers and the group vice presidents—the people close to the market and customers.

Our Strategic Planning Process

Our planning system has three parts: development of key issues for a single division or a group, documentation of the strategic plan itself, and face-to-face discussions between senior officers and operating management. The third part is the most important, especially for the top divisions which total 80 percent of the corporation's economic value. Each year, these divisions develop a five-year plan; other divisions prepare their plans less frequently.

Developing key issues is done primarily by the CFO and the planning department with group and division management. Examples of these issues are: a change in market position, a major decision (e.g., to divest a major operation, double capital investment, or price more aggressively), and a need to run a certain business differently.

Our documentation is short and simple. It consists of about 10 pages, which emphasize strategic direction rather than numbers. The documentation is to spread understanding of each division's direction and to stimulate discussion.

The Leader's Role

It's in the face-to-face discussions that I, as CEO and chairman, can make a contribution. These meetings are normally held at the operating division. They are intense and decision-oriented, not just a recitation of facts and figures already submitted. Being an attentive listener during long days for weeks at a time is extremely demanding but for me, most rewarding. My involvement makes the planning come alive. Division managers know they're going to come face to face with the CEO. These interactions bring a sense of purpose and urgency to the process: operating managers know they're going to be heard; they can argue and get a reaction.

My hope for these sessions is more effective leadership of our operating divisions. In a decentralized company, interaction between the CEO and operating managers is critical. The larger the company, the greater the danger of the CEO being isolated from operating divisions. These planning meetings are the main way for me to understand their strategic direction. It can take a full day to review the key issues and to understand the alternative actions, costs and probable outcomes. Division managers tell us what they need and we try to make decisions right then. Sometimes we have to ask for a further meeting when we're not satisfied. I explain my perspective, giving the division manager and group vice president the opportunity to argue. Our managers have the right—and the responsibility—to argue with the president and with me. And they do, sometimes more often than I'd like, but I go along with it as part of my involvement.

As a CEO, you cannot manage change by sitting in your office and reviewing plans with corporate staff. You have to be there. I believe the planning process is the single best vehicle for a CEO to demonstrate his leadership of the corporation. Our managers have to hear for themselves that I care about the environment, product quality, service reliability, employee communications and, of course, about profits.

Improving the Process

Our general managers used to complain they needed written confirmation of what direction to take as a result of the meetings. So now we designate a planning officer to confirm the final outcome for each division. Whatever the results, they are put into writing immediately.

We continue to improve our process. For example, in the last five years, we set out to understand economic value and how to create and calculate it. It has been an eye-opener. We're now convinced that a company's stock price is directly related to its ability to generate real economic value. Defining economic value as the sum of sales growth, margin improvement, and asset turnover, we're amazed at how much management time typically goes into businesses with negligible economic value.

I take strategic planning seriously. I think about it, plan my calendar around it, and participate in it. Yet I hold operations managers accountable as the real planners. The line manager who balances day-to-day operations with managing for the long term is a candidate for promotion. An understanding of strategy and an ability to handle operating responsibility are the essence of leadership. This results in a dynamic, successful organization. Another result is an irreplaceable sense of personal satisfaction.

Unfulfilled Expectations: Bad Strategy or Poor Implementation?

Raymond V. Gilmartin
President and Chief Executive Officer
Becton Dickinson and Company

Over the past 25 or 30 years, three corporate strategies to create shareholder value have largely failed to fulfill expectations (see box). During this same 30-year period, strategic planning became standard management practice. Yet the failure of these strategies to create shareholder value and the loss of competitive position in many industries to the Japanese raised questions about the value of strategic planning. Did the unfulfilled expectations result from bad strategy, suggesting that the principles of strategic management are inappropriate, or from poor implementation? What will be the strategy for creating value in the 1990s? I draw on my experience as a strategic planner and as president and CEO to respond to these questions.

Becton Dickinson: A Historical Perspective

Becton Dickinson is a global company focused on medical devices and diagnostic systems. International sales, which are currently about 40 percent of our $2 billion revenue, are growing faster than our domestic sales. Our industry is fast, highly competitive, and made up mostly of small companies; Becton Dickinson is an exception. Our growth strategy is to increase share of international growth markets by transferring our qual-

Three Decades of Ineffective Strategic Management

	1960s	1970s	1980s
Strategy to Create Shareholder Value	Diversification through acquisitions, more efficiently managed.	Related diversification for synergy among businesses acquired and developed internally.	Restructuring.
Reasoning Behind Strategy	Avoidance of cyclicality risks.	Whole greater than the sum of the parts.	Parts more valuable than the whole.
Key Management Technology	Management control system.	Strategic management.	Financial engineering.
Key Roles	CEO controls operations using financial measures to assess performance.	Corporate management allocates resources among portfolio of businesses.	Financial markets allocate resources.

ity and cost advantages and to introduce unique new products worldwide. Anticipating market needs with superior products—which are sold at competitive prices and designed or manufactured using proprietary technologies—and building on our existing business and distribution strengths are now the keys to our success.

But in the late 1970s our growth in sales and earnings had slowed significantly despite efforts to shift toward higher growth markets. What caused sales and earnings growth to slow was the federal government changing to reimbursing fixed prices for specific procedures instead of reimbursing the actual cost of treating Medicare patients. The effect on the health care market was immediate: growth slowed dramatically. As hospitals and medical supply distributors delayed spending, so growth in demand for health care supplies slowed. This tougher environment made our intended shift to higher growth markets too risky and costly.

Our strategy development framework allowed us to foresee a rebound in demand and continuing price pressures. Moreover, it gave us four messages:

- *We were too diversified.* While our three industrial businesses were successful, there was no contribution between them and our health care businesses. So we reluctantly divested industrial businesses and focused our resources where we could leverage commonalties in technology, distribution channels and customers.

- *Building too many businesses simultaneously tied up our resources in repairing weakness rather than building on strength.* Payoffs are unlikely when building competitive position from a weak start. So we aggressively discontinued products, wrote down assets, and divested certain products.

- *We had underestimated the resources and time to build new businesses; consequently, we short-changed growth opportunities in diagnostics.* The investment required to change competitive position, or to build a new business, usually exceeds first estimates. So we increased investment in diagnostic start-ups, drawing on funds from the discontinued product lines and from an R&D limited partnership.

- *The final message was that strategy had to be integrated with our management process for effective implementation.* Organizational structure, planning, budgeting and reward systems, management style, skills and staffing all had to be aligned with strategy. Other senior managers and I are directly involved in designing this integration, along with the human resource function.

Acting on these messages returned company profitability to historical levels within three years. From 1986 through 1989, we increased capital and R&D investments to accelerate sales growth. In the next three to five years, we expect steady sales growth and faster growth in profitability that will realize returns on those investments.

Integrating Strategy With Management Process

Integrating strategy with the management process, which we call "strategic human resource management," is to insure we achieve growth and profitability targets and create value by leveraging competitive advantage across business units.

Implementing our strategy of international expansion and worldwide product introductions requires that we anticipate customer needs worldwide; that we balance global scale economies in R&D and manufacturing with responsiveness to local markets; that we shorten the time to market for new products; and that we orchestrate multidivisional distribution and sales activities.

How our organization functions is more important than how it is structured. Accordingly, we are organizing divisions around a single business, eliminating layers and relying on teams to integrate across geography, business and function.

Striving for a high participation led by ideas rather than rank, we keep decision-making close to the market for creativity and quick response. Wide spans of control require a strong cadre of general managers whose jobs have three components: strategy, performance measurement and people. Tight linkage among these is, we believe, the key to organizational effectiveness. We value strategic thinking highly as each general manager is a key strategist. Several general managers have rotated through our small corporate planning staff.

Creating Sustainable Shareholder Value in the 1990s

Let's revisit the questions I raised earlier. What do the failures of past strategies tell us about the contribution of strategic planning to shareholder value and competitive positioning?

I believe that the principles of strategic management are valid, that bad strategy comes from misapplying—or even ignoring—these principles and that poor implementation results from inadequate integration of strategy with the management process.

The challenge for the 1990s has to do with developing a corporate strategy that creates sustainable shareholder value. Corporate strategy must be more than the simple sum of business unit strategies. Growth and profitability together produce shareholder value, as measured by return on equity, and greater profitability comes from greater competitive advantage. Enhancing the business units' competitive advantage is therefore the key to a corporate strategy that creates value.

Market share, relative quality, degree of differentiation and relative cost are key indicators of competitive advantage. Becton Dickinson's corporate strategy is to strengthen these indicators in ways that individual business units cannot. One such way is leveraging commonalties across business units, such as product and manufacturing technologies, channels of distribution, and served markets. For example, managing multidivisional activities at the corporate level lowers the overall cost of doing business with us and improves service, producing economic benefits to distributors that no one division could provide.

Leveraging commonalties requires integration: across geography for global advantage, across units for channel or customer advantage, and across functions for quality and cost advantage. Such integration is difficult for most companies to realize. Thus I expect CEOs will become more involved in integrating strategy and management processes, and that the role of human resources will expand. Using the strategic planning process as the command and control system allows senior management to manage this integration, supporting the corporate strategy that I believe will create shareholder value in the 1990s: leveraging competitive advantage across business units.

People Power: A Global Challenge for the 1990s[1]

Richard U. Jelinek
Vice President
General Electric Company

Richard U. Jelinek
Vice President
General Electric Company

Before joining General Electric, I spent 10 years consulting with four of their biggest businesses to determine what makes people at all levels give or withhold their best, why they love or just tolerate a company, and what remarkable things happen when people are challenged, trusted and empowered.

The Power Shift of the '90s: People Empowered

The two major movements of the 1980s—restructuring and globalization—came from executive suites, not from employee suggestion boxes. Restructuring was imperative for industrial America to survive in an increasingly globalized, intensely competitive economy. Companies focused more on portfolios than on people, fired more than hired, and invested more in machines than in skills. Competitive realities inspired fear in the work force giving management the power to act.

The top-down dynamics are ending. The '70s was the decade of the manager; the '80s the decade of the leader. The '90s is shaping up to be the decade of the leader-and-the-team, of power shared not withheld, of power balanced not imposed.

Power is shifting from the board room to the workplace where value is added and wealth created. Power and career security will go to employees with adaptable minds and flexible skills. Power and profits will go to companies smart enough to make their workplaces, work practices and training programs the most attractive. Power and wealth will go to nations wise enough to invest in children, schools and skills. Adapting to the shift toward people power, while maintaining competitive rigor, is today's central human resource challenge.

[1] This speech draws significantly on arguments and language developed by General Electric's Senior Vice President, Frank P. Doyle, in his paper "People-Power: The Global Human Resource Challenge for the '90s," *The Columbia Journal of World Business*, Spring/Summer 1990.

Demographics, Technology, Productivity

Demographic trends are one major factor of employee strength. An aging population and a contracting number of work force entrants bring the U.S. labor force growth rate to barely one percent over the next decade. No longer will too many people chase too few jobs, except the low- or non-skilled jobs, which will be scarcer as U.S. companies move to higher value-added work. The crunch of too many jobs chasing too few qualified people will, in the mid- or late-'90s, cause retirement age to be pushed out. And for the educated and trainable, anticipated shortages of skilled labor will make it an employees' market.

Technology is also causing more concerted "people power." With personal computers on every desk and factories resembling offices, the people whom Peter Drucker calls "knowledge workers" will have both autonomy and mobility. Linked PCs and workstations make open communications a way of life. Thus knowledge workers' access to information will exceed the company's power to contain it. The days of withholding information as a form of hierarchical power are over.

Change in the sources of competitive advantage and productivity growth are also causing power to shift. The globalization of high-technology—at least among North America, Europe and East Asia—renders technology advances a less vital source of competitive advantage. Emerging wage parity within each geographic bloc is reducing labor cost as a competitive factor. Productivity will come from work which results in added value for the customer.

The Shifting Balance of Power in the Workplace: Mobility and Independence

Deriving personal security from their skills, "knowledge workers" will have options in competitive labor markets. Companies will have to strive to attract and retain needed workers or the best will seek companies offering the best growth environments, flexible benefits and generous training. Loyalty will be earned, not owed. Smart people who feel unduly constrained and without influence will move from employer to employer.

No longer will management empower the work force. Work forces will not only have the power; they will exercise it. Management should accept and act on the proposition that winning in the '90s will depend on a total organizational commitment to retain smart, highly mobile people.

People Power and Productivity Growth

With the grueling pace of global competition, and the hardships of recession, it might seem that the demands of people power are coming at a bad time. But people power is less a threat than an opportunity when linked to productivity.

For most companies, including GE, the traditional route to productivity growth has been to attack cost structures and head count through restructuring, downsizing, and investing in product and process technology. This "hardware" approach has merits but misses the "software" side of productivity: productivity growth through people brought about by transforming the company culture and work environment.

Advantage will go to lean and agile companies; to flat organizations; to managers who listen and leaders who communicate; to liberated and entrepreneurial cultures; and to people technically and culturally fluent and flexible. As the power structure of highly directive, unilateral decision-making erodes, the successful business leaders of the '80s will not necessarily win in the '90s. They will find that employee fear and acceptance of competitive reality aren't enough to secure managerial authority.

Managers will need to be leaders of teams and have the self-confidence to share. They will need to listen as much as command and to sell more than impose. They

will need to be innovators and communicators, responding to employees' concerns about workplace, environment and training in ways that balance power rather than abdicate it.

Employers seeking a stable and productive work force will offer healthy and satisfying work environments with high, but competitive, pay levels and with benefits that are owned and portable. They will invest in more employee training at all levels, accepting the risk that trained employees may then leave for another company. Smart employers will learn to lead better, emphasizing openness, involvement, diversity, and better work and workplaces.

From Bureaucracy to Content

People power compels companies to liberate people to do only the important work. Seeing this as an opportunity, we at GE are encouraging our businesses to adopt the principles of speed, simplicity and self-confidence. Technological prowess will remain vital, but people power will be paramount. Having restructured businesses and taken out people in the '80s is not enough for us: Our major emphasis in the '90s will be on changing the company's culture.

If the '80s were about getting waste out, the '90s will be about putting value in. We have, therefore, embarked on a decade-long crusade to make each of the 300,000 employees in our company an engine of our success rather than a passenger. The project, called Work-Out, is designed to energize and empower our whole work force from top management to the shop floor. All across the world it's open season on the bureaucracy, autocracy and waste that get in the way of our ultimate objective: providing customer value and service. We put people into a room away from their traditional roles and routines and encourage them to challenge and criticize. We're hearing indications of change from all corners of the company (see box).

Voices of Change at GE

We hear less of...	We hear more of...
"We don't trust the company or the other department."	"Trust is building."
"Our opinions don't count."	"Our opinions are beginning to matter."
"We're treated like just a pair of hands."	"We're treated like a respected resource."
"We're blamed for all the quality problems."	"We're blaming the process for the quality problems." •
"We don't know how the pieces fit together."	"We're starting to understand the importance of our piece."

After two years, we've learned some lessons. Early on we found out that empowerment starts with candor and sharing—two essential building blocks of trust. Equally important is that management treat the work force as the experts they are. We're learning that what drives organizational change is visible change in the leader's behavior—indeed in every manager's behavior—not just in their rhetoric. And we're learning to share credit for success and accountability for failure.

The Corporate Response: Beyond Zero

For a company to benefit from people power, it has to take immediate action, starting where people power can have the greatest impact: in the workplace and the marketplace.

The most successful companies will be those that elevate their commitment to human resources before they have to, just as companies that restructured and globalized before they had to in the '80s entered the '90s on strong competitive terms. Firms that invest now in employee growth will gain the services of the best knowledge workers while companies that wait will be defeated by competition. Companies that change early will make people power work for them instead of being its victim.

But can companies afford the risk in 1991? Can we take the time to recognize and respond to people power? Can we afford to abandon top-down habits in a year of war and recession? These are good questions but they can evoke the wrong answers.

My answer begins with an analogy. Restructuring, downsizing and delayering started in the tough early- to mid-'80s. But that top-down rigor wasn't suddenly suspended when the good years came. The best companies understood that strategic focus, organizational leanness and overall cost competitiveness would remain relevant in the boom years. The best companies understood the underlying forces. Similarly, the underlying forces that are rebalancing power—the changing demographic facts, technological tools and sources of competitive advantage—became visible in the late '80s. These forces will continue to drive the empowering trend.

Keeping a long-term focus—even in recession—reduces the temptation to fall back on the tried and the tested, to go back on the attack, to take costs down as demand shrinks. Taking costs down in 1991 is smart; putting value in throughout the decades will be smarter still.

We must overcome a criticism of corporate America: that we only think, plan and act short-term. We not only know better, we *do* better. Balancing short- and long-term demands is what strategic management is all about.

Vision and Values: Leading the Way to Success

Charles L. Bowerman

Senior Vice President, Petroleum Products
Phillips Petroleum Company

These days, it's important to focus on solid principles of good management that are more than just "flavor of the month" improvement ideas. We hear a lot about leadership, about the importance of a leader's vision, and about values. Whatever terms you use—"mission" or "strategic intent" for "vision"; "principles of performance" or "code of ethics" for "values"—these concepts should be more than just the latest management fad. A vision is really a clear sense of direction defining the organization's purpose and what it's trying to accomplish. Values are really about the behavior of the organization—how it acts and why. Seen in this light, it's clear that these concepts are fundamental and critical to success.

Having a vision and a set of values serves a practical purpose. Without an overall objective work lacks meaning. People lose motivation and performance deteriorates. Indicating to people throughout the organization that what they do makes a difference is an essential part of leadership.

The Effective Vision

To be effective, a vision must be practical and understandable, not mystical or intangible. Precise enough to provide guidance, the vision must be broad enough to encourage initiative and to inspire commitment. NASA's mission to land Americans on the moon and bring them safely back to earth is a good example. That mission generated tremendous commitment with the result that people accomplished what seemed impossible. Another good example is Apple Computer's vision to start a revolution in the way that people process information and do their work. Effective visions rarely include numbers. And they never work unless they're put into practice.

The vision must tie in with shared values. For example, successful retailing organizations seek genuinely friendly people; sales experience is secondary. The reasoning is that you can teach people about business but you can't teach them to be nice. The vision must also be believable. We all want to have pride in our work and to do so we have to believe in what we're doing.

Making the Vision Real

For people to believe in what they're doing, the vision must be made real to them. This happens when you demonstrate how specific strategies support the vision. It's for the organization's leaders to initiate communication throughout the organization—not by issuing marching orders but by explaining, listening and building team spirit. Teamwork is essential: No one-man band can match a symphony orchestra. But every orchestra needs a conductor.

An effective leader makes sure that strategies support the vision in a realistic way. Moreover, the effective leader sets an example. The leader's actions are a model for the rest of the organization to follow. This is a matter of substance, not of style. Actions really do speak louder than words.

Vision Precedes Action to Get Results

A champion golfer recommends you first visualize the ball exactly where you want it to be, picture it in flight, and then consider the swing to turn these previous images into reality. Similarly, business success starts with somebody's vision, which then motivates other people to transform it into reality. As managers who lead, the vision we define and share will largely determine our organization's success.

How to Get the Organization to Think and Manage Strategically

Andrew G. Bodnar
Senior Vice President, Strategic Management
Bristol-Myers Squibb Pharmaceutical Group

Going from planning strategically to thinking strategically to managing strategically is the challenge. Formed in a recent merger, Bristol-Myers Squibb needed to regain some centralized management of our strategy development and implementation. However, centralization raises questions about how to balance and organize the roles of line managers and strategic managers.

Strategic Product Planning's Role and Responsibilities

Managers in Strategic Product Planning have several roles. Like all research-driven companies, Bristol-Myers Squibb has two cultures. People in R&D have a different, longer-term focus than do commercial and operating people. One of our roles is to help integrate these views. The company is in various therapeutic areas to which we bring an overall sense of direction. By looking across these areas to market franchises, we make sure new areas are explored in spite of vested interests. Providing input into the therapeutic area strategies and R&D priorities, we ensure that they are consistent with Pharmaceutical Group and corporate goals.

Our responsibilities differ for compounds in development and in commercialization. For compounds still in R&D, we lead preparation of worldwide strategies and other pre-launch plans. For compounds already on the market, we ensure communication between countries, working with local marketing groups to identify new claims and dosage forms and to determine patent expiration strategy—a critical issue in pharmaceuticals.

Notice what soft words I've used, such as "provide input" and "ensure communication." This is important:

Our job is to inject intellectual vitality but not to run things. Neither Strategic Product Planning nor strategic management determines corporate strategy. Instead, we work with the senior managers who come up with strategies, which we bring together into an overall corporate strategy.

How Our Strategic Product Planning Process Works

The first step is to define worldwide product strategies and objectives. R&D then develops tactical plans, as do worldwide marketing and manufacturing.

Subgroups of Strategic Product Planning are responsible for specific therapeutic areas. Project teams are each responsible for a particular compound. Each subgroup has medical and business people who unify R&D and marketing views into a coherent strategy. Our multidisciplinary team approach is important. The subgroups do not displace line management's role or contribution. Rather, we make sure line functions achieve consensus. Senior people represent R&D, marketing and manufacturing interests on each project team; each team is limited to only one compound. Even the next compound within a therapeutic area is beyond the boundary of a team's project.

A multidisciplinary team also makes sure we have a coherent long-term strategy for each therapeutic area. When a new compound comes out of R&D, a therapeutic area strategy team determines initial regulatory strategies and what market needs are likely to be years from now. Once proposed and approved, the strategy for a new compound goes to a project team for implementation. A strategy team doesn't dictate detailed actions, such as clinical studies. But a strategy team does make sure there is agreement that the company is properly positioned in a particular therapeutic area and should be in one area rather than another, and that a specific compound should go forward with certain attributes. It is generally understood that such decisions aren't reversed from one year to the next. This approach makes sure all the relevant people are involved as early as possible and what's decided on is implemented.

These arrangements are complex; some people say more complex than necessary. The arrangements were designed to meet a real need: to insure we have a coherent strategy that all elements in the company subscribe to and that is executed.

When Is It a "Strategy"?

Henry DeNero
Director
McKinsey & Company, Inc.

One can define and discuss strategy in general terms all day long but the test of a good strategy is whether it leads to improved business performance. Therefore, what constitutes an effective strategy varies enormously with the situation.

Let's look at the elements of any strategy. The general definition I think best is: "an integrated set of actions designed to develop competitive advantage." The key considerations in developing a business strategy are to:

- create a set of distinct actions that make up one integrated, consistent whole
- focus on delivering value to customers
- differentiate from competitors
- recognize tradeoffs between gaining advantages for the company and affecting overall industry attractiveness

Appropriate Strategies

Now let's look at what is an appropriate strategy. The type of strategy—whether it is offensive or defensive, whether it applies at the company or business unit level—is less important than its suitability in a particular situation. Here are two examples of how strategy varies with the situation:

Compaq's challenge with personal computers called for addressing the competition, in this case IBM. Compaq had to position itself as IBM-compatible and find a way to create an advantage for users of the IBM PCs. Thus, Compaq emphasized portables and lower prices to attack IBM's position.

A defense contractor today faced with a 30 to 40 percent decline in projected demand would downsize and streamline product development and manufacturing.

Good Strategies

In addition to being appropriate, a good strategy must anticipate—not react. It's also likely to be incremental; that is, it builds selectively on an organization's strengths while recognizing its limitations. Some examples:

Avery, holding the lion's share of the pressure-sensitive label business in the office supply industry, came under attack by three competitors. One of the competitors was owned by 3M, which introduced removable labels for file folders. In response, Avery followed with a defensive strategy: minimizing the loss of value (not of share) by stepping up its rate of new product introduction; creating a second brand for the most price-sensitive market segment; negotiating improved service relationships with major distributors; and modifying its pricing to reflect total sales volume to each account. Avery retained most of its market share without substantial price erosion, and 3M decided to withdraw from the pressure-sensitive label business.

TRW's credit reporting business employed a variety of strategies to improve its basic product and expanded into value-added services, such as providing credit-scoring models to midsized banks.

ARCO, a Southern California-based company in the retail business, pursued a series of successful strategies. Its low-price, no-credit-card strategy resulted in a market share increase. ARCO's AM/PM Minimart combines a walk-in convenience store with a self-serve, cash-only gasoline station format that has appeal to a broad market segment. And ARCO has introduced an "environmentally sensitive" gasoline.

Finally, whether improved business performance is the result of good strategy or of good market timing is sometimes difficult to ascertain.

From Informal to Formal Planning

William S. Banowsky
Executive Vice President and Director
National Medical Enterprises

Founded in 1969, National Medical Enterprises is now a $4 billion company and our stock is at an all-time high. During our first decade, we planned informally. Then we formalized our planning, focusing the company and improving profitability.

The Transition from Informal to Formal Planning

Our company was founded by three people who are still providing vital leadership. They set out to build a for-profit health care company when non-profit organizations were producing disastrous results. Experienced in this industry, the founders defined a niche. Their vision was to provide the highest quality care in the community, to have the cleanest, newest and best hospitals. Back then, their strategies included avoiding types of care with low profit potential, such as trauma and indigent care. Another strategy was to retain local identity and autonomy.

Many health care companies that started around the same time ran into hard times. So did we. This prompted us to establish a strategic and financial planning function, headed by an executive vice president who is on the board. As a result, we replaced our historical growth strategy—acquire and diversify—with a more selective and profit-oriented approach. For example, we bought a psychiatric company as an entry into the fastest-growing part of the industry—psychiatric and physical rehabilitation and substance abuse treatment. These specialty institutions now provide almost 50 percent of our revenues. We also divested and restructured the whole company. We sold operations that lacked adequate profit potential such as home health care, construction and distribution, and insurance. Recognizing that the original vision—to be the highest quality provider in each community—required direct, rather than contract, management, we divested further. For example, we reduced our acute care facilities to 36 from 52. By divesting, we strengthened our margins significantly.

Implementing such moves effectively takes courage. Our chairman had to make tough decisions and lead prompt action—and did. This paid off. For example, disposing of one-third of the company almost doubled shareholder value in a 36-month period. Yet our stock was still undervalued. The chairman acted to change this by spinning off our convalescent operations as a separate entity. Though a viable business, long-term care has lower profit margins than our other divisions. The spin-off was completed in 1989, and our stock price increased further.

Looking Forward

While the health care industry is facing some major issues, we are well-positioned to take advantage of them. These issues include political considerations, cost pressures, demographic trends and patient access to care. Our vision and strategies specify that we are to be the best, have the finest locations and let genuine autonomy work in the communities we serve. This autonomy is key: we're constantly pressing our operating entities to tell us where the markets are, what's happening in the marketplace, and what actions they propose. We are changing our strategies to reflect operating realities.

For the long-term, our strategy has a philosophical side. We're in the business of helping people. This philosophy shows in various ways. For example, philanthropy is part of our long-term corporate strategy. So we recently rented the Los Angeles Forum for a performance of the Moscow Circus to benefit a child-abuse organization. My company is trying to give back. Doing so means acknowledging that our employees—the people who actually provide care—are the real heart of the company.

Strategy and the Board of Directors

Richard T. Bueschel
Chairman
Northern Equities, Inc.

I am currently a director of small technology companies with annual sales of $1 million to $30 million. My prior experience was as CEO of startup companies and companies in transition; often, these are companies with problems.

The board involvement at these companies is often more intense than at larger companies. Typically, they are small working boards consisting of five to eight directors, including four to six outside directors.

The board is there to provide counsel. In effect they are outside consultants to top management. And while board meetings may be as few as four a year, the board members are on call and usually consulted and involved on a much more frequent schedule.

The Board's Responsibilities... and Management's

But while this board may, and should, provide counsel, give advice, review plans, oversee the use of corporate resources, and, in some cases, suggest or make changes in management, they should not set strategy. Management is responsible for setting strategy and implementing it. The board should review, question and evaluate strategy, and make suggestions. The board, of course, is responsible for insisting that management develop a strategy and change the strategy as external and internal conditions dictate. No strategy can be static. It must be reviewed regularly and frequently. It is a living document, not something to be stuffed in a drawer and forgotten.

How does the board carry out its responsibility in insuring that top management has and implements a strategic plan? In part it depends on top management. The board should know who in management has participated in developing the strategic document. I like to meet these people and be assured that a plurality has accepted the strategy. Adequate time to thoroughly understand the strategy and its ramifications should be allowed.

In addition, the smaller company usually does not have a formal planning department or even a planning function; strategic planning is almost always headed by the CEO. It is much more of an art than a science.

Therefore, there can be a tendency to overstep and offer a greater amount of strategic advice than is appropriate. This can be compounded, especially in startups, by an inexperienced management team that accepts or solicits more strategic advice than is appropriate. The danger is that the strategy is no longer perceived to be management's. The company's strategy becomes set by consensus, which includes the board of directors, and the CEO is no longer responsible. The board can no longer be objective in questioning and evaluating strategy.

The board's proper role is to require management to set strategy, evaluate, question and critique it, see to it that the company strategy will build a competitive enterprise, see that action is taken and the strategy is carried out, and review, question and insure that the strategy adapts to changes in the marketplace, economy, competition and other forces. In summary, the board's role is to continually review strategy and its implementation. This means significant milestones must be reestablished and remet, with changes and new opportunities taken into account to insure that the strategy is carried out.

The biggest problem often is getting management to sit down and address the need for strategy that goes beyond saying, "We want to be a $200 million company." Next, is to understand the difference between strategic planning and long-range planning.

Example One

One company set a strategy of pursuing related medium-tech markets. In time it was apparent that one of the company's most profitable businesses in specialized connectors was becoming more generic and moving towards the lower end of the technology spectrum. What had been unique five years ago wasn't now. That segment of the market was no longer a small niche: It was attracting larger players.

The company's strengths and weaknesses were analyzed with the focus on this group and how it fit with the overall strategy. It was concluded that this segment of the business would continue to become more generic and would require substantial capital investment to compete with larger firms that were entering this once comfortable market. Subsequently, the business was sold to a larger competitor while it was still very profitable.

What role did the board play? It prodded the company to examine and reassess strategy, even though management hated to sell such a profitable division.

Example Two

In another instance a company began by developing a global authoring program for computer imaging systems. They were ahead of their time and had only limited success. A new strategy was adopted in which they narrowed their sights and built on their expertise in the systems area to develop specific applications in the adult learning field. Interestingly, the exposure that they are now getting from their applications programs is opening up opportunities for them to sell the authoring system on various computer platforms.

In both of these cases management set and implemented the strategy, and the board of directors actively participated in reviewing, questioning, challenging and providing input to the strategy. But in the end it is management's strategy and management has to implement and stand by it.

Planning for Action in the Smaller Company

Robba L. Benjamin
President and Chief Operating Officer
TransWestern Publishing

In contrast to the previous speaker's planning organization, TransWestern Publishing has no full-time planning staff and produces a one-page plan. TransWestern Publishing, a subsidiary of U S WEST, is a sales channel, packager, publisher and distributor of white-and-yellow-page telephone directories. We generate revenues through the sale of advertising space. This is a highly competitive business and the directories themselves are considered a low-interest product category. That is, consumers and businesses take for granted the features and benefits of the product.

Although we are one of the largest independent publishers of yellow pages and the only publisher of nationwide presence, we are a small company in a mature industry dominated by big players. Being small, we lack time, financial resources, staff, and formal business management training. Survival is our main challenge, and the way we plan reflects this.

Having come from a large company—an $8 billion savings bank—before joining U S WEST as President of TransWestern, I had experience in designing and managing large and small company planning approaches. Based on my experience, I believe large companies can learn from the smaller ones.

Pragmatic Planning

When I arrived at TransWestern, the company had just lost roughly $27 million on $50 million in revenues and had a severely negative cash flow. The business plan was not well documented; there was very little historical information, and communication with employees was sporadic. Most employees apparently didn't know the company was losing money. We also had operating problems. We didn't know how many customers we had and whether we had sent them bills or been paid. Our billing process serving 80,000 customers was entirely

manual. Our many acquisitions—between 1985 and 1988 we had acquired 15 separate companies publishing more than 150 directories—had not been fully integrated. As a result, we had at least 15 different ideas of what the product actually was and how to price, sell and manufacture it.

To focus our turnaround, I developed a simple visual plan which is producing results (see exhibit on page 27). The reasoning behind this planning approach is to: a) focus on one step at a time or, in other words, to walk before we run, and to b) communicate the business in the same simple terms to all audiences. The plan has three additive stages.

Stage one is about generating positive cash flow. To do that, you start with a strategy to restore confidence. The purpose of planning is to enable correct action. Correct action doesn't occur if employees, customers or owners lack confidence. To know what action to take, you must also gather data about the business and its customers, install basic control systems and work on the cost side of the business—the other main components of stage one strategy. The goal of stage one is to produce positive cash flow—the life blood of our business.

The second stage, which overlaps with the first, is about building a profitable base business. Once basic measurement and control mechanisms are in place, you must increase productivity—do more with less without diminishing confidence, quality or cash flow. Working on price/value relationships and selectively pruning our portfolio so that the company will reliably produce a profit is our principal focus. Within the last year, we have added a senior marketing executive to build our marketing systems, and are investing heavily in market research and customer requirements knowledge as preparation for the next stage. We know we can make our core business work.

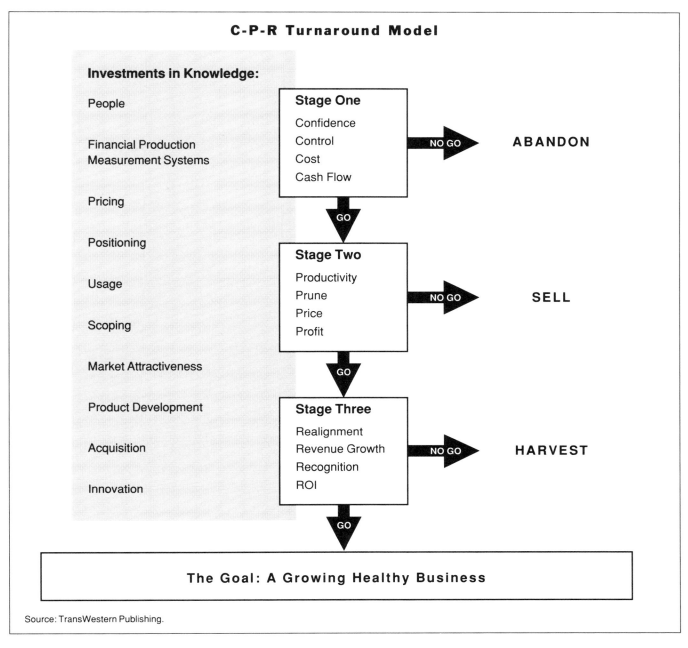

C-P-R Turnaround Model

Investments in Knowledge:

People

Financial Production
Measurement Systems

Pricing

Positioning

Usage

Scoping

Market Attractiveness

Product Development

Acquisition

Innovation

Stage One
Confidence
Control
Cost
Cash Flow

NO GO → **ABANDON**

GO

Stage Two
Productivity
Prune
Price
Profit

NO GO → **SELL**

GO

Stage Three
Realignment
Revenue Growth
Recognition
ROI

NO GO → **HARVEST**

GO

The Goal: A Growing Healthy Business

Source: TransWestern Publishing.

The third stage is about developing a sustainable and sizable return on investment. In it you add focus on expansion of your market position through product or market development. The objective is to continue to achieve the return on investment you've targeted and to create a growing, healthy company.

Common Understanding and Goals

One of the best ways to deploy this three-stage approach is to tell and show everybody everything as a way to build knowledge and a sense of involvement. Our managers currently spend 10-12 days a year specifically increasing their knowledge of the economics of the business. Our practice is to include everyone in

what the company is doing, explain company goals, and show people how they can contribute. I believe that giving employees a specific understanding of how, when and where they contribute to our success as well as how others contribute to the bigger picture increases confidence and output and builds satisfaction and loyalty.

As our employees learned, so did we. The first time we exposed employees to this approach, they developed their individual financial plans and budgets in the more conventional top-down manner. In our first year together, we missed our financial targets by a wide margin. Together we found out that none of us knows how all the pieces fit together to produce profits. As a result, we now constantly teach employees how the business works by taking actual business problems and solving them in small teams using facts and data, process definition, brainstorming, financial modeling, and so on. Managers solve actual problems in real time together as a teaching technique, a team builder, and as a profit strategy. We found, for example, that while we all talked about contribution margin, it meant different things to different people. The need for common language indicated we had to break down the business as simply as possible and focus on how things work. Our efforts focus on the means as much as the ends as a method to shorten the time and cost of making business improvements. We seek to reduce the time our employees spend second guessing and trying to figure out the system.

Defining the process we use, for example, to make a sale—the steps, timing and costs—has been very productive. Working on cross-discipline teams builds a common understanding, builds confidence and knowledge, saves implementation time, and reduces errors. It has produced many good ideas throughout the organization, which are essential because our resources for external consultants are so limited. From a financial standpoint, use of this method has contributed to an improvement in cash flow equal to 50 percent of our revenue, to a decrease in sales and manufacturing time cycles of more than 25 percent, and to resumed growth of our customer base. Our sales increases are currently more than 30 percent higher than the industry rate, attesting to growing customer confidence.

After two years of focused effort, we now feel ready to render simple statements about our mission, goals and guiding principles. People need a mission they can understand, believe in and translate into action. We've found that being less scientific and more philosophical in this aspect of business planning encourages commitment and predisposition to action and teamwork. We believe that the broadest definition of a customer is the person who receives your output. That being the case, our mission is simply to make our customers' dreams come true. It is important to us that the mission statement "work" for all "customers"—employees, owners, advertisers and consumers; that it keeps us going through tough times; and that it helps to give perspective to our annual budgeting process without unnecessarily constraining innovation.

To further refine our emphasis on continuous improvement we are building a system whereby everyone—employees and managers alike—can monitor their own activities and outcomes. We have linked our performance evaluation system and our financial systems to company goals. This year, for the first time, our key managers' incentive compensation plan is completely tied to the company's performance. We are also focusing on the products that are most profitable and beginning to benchmark ourselves against other companies within and outside our industry.

Our strategies are very simple: build quality, simplify the business, differentiate the product, and make the customers happy. The keys to making our strategies work through planning are to communicate continually, thoroughly, and elegantly to all audiences; to building knowledge; to encourage involvement and action; and to maintain our focus on walking well before we run.

Mobilizing a Global Plan

Thomas M. Liptak
Kane-Liptak Associates
IBM Corporation (Retired)
Vice President, Organization and Management Systems

After decades of losing market share and even whole industries to foreign competition, we still don't seem to be truly global competitors. Few industries have joined the export sector in the last 10 years.

Reluctantly, I conclude that we are rationalizing our inadequacies. Other countries actually have greater problems than the United States, yet they do better internationally than we do.

My theory is that historically and culturally we have not been a trading nation because we didn't need to be—we had a huge, single-language market and only started shipping outside the United States to meet pent-up demand that couldn't be filled by foreign industry. Fundamentally, we were meeting foreign demand with our surplus products. Volume was more important than quality and products tailored to other countries.

Will America ever get its act together? I'm not sure that we will, but I do have some recommendations. After extensive research involving hundreds of companies, I believe that they don't really organize themselves to be global competitors.

Recommendations for Global Effectiveness

Having an international department or giving product managers worldwide scope isn't enough. The principles behind organizing for global effectiveness are the same for large and small companies. My recommendations are:

1. Assign specific responsibility for understanding your international market opportunities and competitors. Ad hoc, low-priority, part-time efforts don't work. Selecting where to do business is essential. Many efforts have been abandoned because people tried to boil the ocean and drowned in a sea of frustration and piles of data. Typically, a company need track only a half dozen markets and competitors. These efforts must be part of your planning systems and resource allocation decisions at a high level so they won't be overwhelmed by operating pressures.

2. Decide early and communicate broadly the balance of power between foreign markets and centralized product management. Specifying authority areas avoids wasting management time. For example, who decides which product goes to which country? If it's product management, what is the role of the country other than pure sales and services? Country management should approve product design, determine its own pricing, and even procure competitors' products to satisfy its customers' needs. Foreign operations should be profit centers.

3. Define measurements that clearly support what you're trying to do. In a global, market-driven world this means product management has to be subject to measures of overseas activities, such as market share, quality and customer satisfaction. Secondary measurements, such as product cost and speed to marketplace should be against worldwide competitors. IBM's competitive analysis has long been watching Fujitsu, Hitachi, NEC and Siemens as well as Unisys and Control Data.

4. Be prepared to hire, trust, and promote foreign nationals. People from Iowa will never understand why the housewife in Osaka—or the small businessman in Stuttgart—has a unique need. This level of understanding is what being market driven is all about. It's also easier for foreign nationals to understand other matters, such as financing, sourcing, advertising and sales promotion, and market channels.

Most companies are in global competition whether they want to be or not. You can play defense only or set out to become a global competitor. Doing so successfully requires organizing to get the job done. The alternative is to join the list of companies that are fading away.

Achieving Central-Regional Communication

Steve Barnett
Director of Product and Market Strategy
Nissan North America

Centralization in global strategic planning runs head on into regional thinking. As each region has its own vocabulary, the issue is how to bridge communication gaps.

Initially, Nissan sold cars in the United States that were made in Japan according to designs modified to meet U.S. regulations. We then adopted the "lead country" concept which meant certain cars were built solely for major countries, of which the United States is one. But the lead country concept resulted in expending a huge amount of resources on cars that lacked global potential. So we adopted a compromise strategy whereby all vehicles should fit at least two markets and resource allocation, manufacturing and distribution are global. Nissan North America (NNA) was formed as the area headquarters in 1990. My department is therefore still young; it reports directly to the global strategic planning department in Tokyo.

Different Concepts and Vocabularies

Nissan is a good example of the discrepancy between global and regional thinking and between centralized and regional vocabularies. In Japan, people shop within very narrow economic bands for their cars whereas in the United States there is significant cross-shopping. Most of us here shop not only within our price band but above and below it. For example, Maxima is cross-shopped with Accord, which is significantly cheaper, and with Legend, which is significantly more expensive. I have said many times that segmenting our market according to U.S. consumers rather than Japan's categories would reveal opportunities. The response I get is that people at headquarters think in terms of those categories. But repetition works; we now segment differently in Japan and the United States.

In Japan the central vocabulary is based on a model where truth is reasoned and absolute. The introductory advertising campaign for the Infiniti was the result of such reasoning. The regional vocabulary, however, is more ambiguous and less uncertain. Communication between the two is difficult.

Seen in this light, strategic planning has to do with meshing vocabularies. For example, when planning from the central standpoint, you want single-point forecasting—one number. We intentionally avoid that because single-point forecasting lacks credibility. We also avoid band-width forecasting because both in Japan and the United States someone simply picks the midpoint. So we use the Royal Dutch Shell scenario planning instead—two or three different perspectives fleshed out in detail. Our aim is to create a bridging vocabulary between centralized certainty and regional uncertainty.

Effective Communication Tools

The ability to bridge vocabularies is increasingly important, and we do it in different ways. We've created videos on many important topics and I take them to Japan so people can actually see them. Actually seeing—through graphics and diagrams—is more effective than reading or hearing words. We also tell compelling stories. As a strategic planner, I am half scientist and half raconteur. I've used Zen stories I read in college because people in Japan recognize them and understand.

Using such communications tools, I am now introducing the idea of "delightful quality." Quality in the auto business is taken for granted so you now have to do more to delight the consumer. I am creating videos to show why delight is becoming more important to the consumer. The challenge for my group—and for other global companies—is to develop ways of bridging communication gaps so as to make strategic planning effective.

Global Expansion Takes a Measured Pace

Harvey Leong

Executive Vice President, Planning and Development
NYNEX International Company

Companies go global because that's where the money is. Were our U.S. markets growing fast, we would stay here. NYNEX owns and operates the telephone franchise in New York City and in Boston where the growth rate is 2-3 percent a year. Overseas markets are growing 10-20 percent. With 25 percent of U.S. international calls coming out of the NYNEX region, which includes a world financial center, NYNEX has a source of global differentiation.

Throughout the world governments are realizing that telecommunications is the backbone of economic development in the next century, and are acting accordingly. Privatization and introduction of competition are the themes. For example, the UK took two steps, privatizing British Telecom and introducing franchise licenses. Telefonos de Mexico was privatized a while ago; Australia is privatizing now and New Zealand already has. Singapore, Taiwan, Thailand, Indonesia, Hungary and Poland are all considering privatization and the letting of licenses to attract capital.

Building the Foundation First

NYNEX's core strength is operating networks, both telecommunications and information, but what we really have to offer is a set of skills built over 100 years. Yet before we can exploit them, we have to have a public franchise and that means working with local governments.

For us, therefore, overseas expansion starts with building relationships. We pick markets throughout the world that our top management is comfortable with, avoiding, for example, Africa, the Middle East, and India. The countries we do go to are the most competitive as they're the easiest ones to enter. The relationships we build are with telecommunications authorities and with industrial companies as partners. These com-

panies understand the government framework, the labor situation, the market, and the culture. Their knowledge complements our telecommunications skills.

As we build alliances, we invest. Six years ago we had two offices, in Geneva and in Hong Kong, and have since added others as the level of business warranted. We are now selectively adding appropriate technical people in each region to meet local demands in a timely fashion.

Another initiative is building the integration skill so critical in the telecommunications business. For a network to meet the needs of specific customers in a specific country hardware, software and networking skills have to be integrated. With software development centers in Ireland and in Manila, we are also building our software design capabilities through acquisition and alliances with other companies.

Developmental efforts support future expansion. In the UK, there is a telecom license associated with cable television which gives us a chance to see if the combination of entertainment and telecommunications is a viable business and to test new technologies. We're also building a network of companies, throughout the United States and the world, that specialize in banking software because this gives us entree into communications.

Long-Term View

Any planner would like a clean slate where you can assess the situation, build strategies, tactics and plans, and implement them. And in a way, NYNEX had an opportunity like that. As competition increased and our market slowed economically, we could go further afield. But expanding globally is a slow process. You have to take the time to learn, to go a step at a time, to work with the sovereignty, other industries, other companies and the local labor force. All this is groundwork before you get to the customer. There are no shortcuts.

Turning Vision into Reality

James C. Chapman
President and Chief Executive Officer
Outboard Marine Corporation

Vision and values are usually seen differently abroad, which presents the global corporation with a challenge: how to get all of its employees to share the same vision. A corporation's greatest resource is its people; unifying their efforts through a common vision is the key to achieving worldwide success.

Communicating the Vision

It is critical to our success that our global vision is understood and embraced, both in our international and domestic operations. Our vision is to be "the company that takes the world boating" and to achieve worldwide leadership through the quality and diversity of our product line, the reach and effectiveness of our sales organization, and the teamwork and commitment of our people. Overseas markets account for about 30 percent of our sales and offer us opportunities for growth.

Communicating information about the corporate mission, objectives and tactics is important but not enough. For people to embrace the vision, they have to see that it is worth striving for, that the corporation values their contribution, and that they will benefit from working on the vision. You must get people to identify with—and believe—that the vision has more to do with what management does than what management says. One way we demonstrate that employees are part of the vision is to delegate to them the authority and responsibility for turning it into reality.

Our ten principal international facilities are responsible for more than sales and service. These facilities are entrusted with realizing our corporate vision. They have total regional authority for marketing and, where appropriate, for product design and manufacturing.

Delegating the Authority

The way we delegate authority brings us ever closer to realizing our vision. In many parts of the world, boats and motors are used more for making a living than for recreation. For example, throughout Latin America and the Far East, outboard-powered boats are widely used by commercial fishermen. In Singapore and Thailand, fishermen use a traditional boat design for which standard outboard motors are unsuitable. Our regional marketing people were convinced fishermen would not change their boats, though it would only take five minutes, and so exercised the authority they'd been given. Our marketers' initiative resulted in a success for the corporation.

Another example has to do with manufacturing in the United States. While many of our engines are manufactured abroad, we plan to continue to make most of them in this country. Again we delegated authority, this time for improving competitiveness through employee involvement programs. Whether in plants or in offices, people have a say in how they will achieve functional objectives and contribute to corporate goals.

By delegating authority we are demonstrating to people throughout the company how they are part of the vision. This encourages them to embrace the vision as their own and work towards achieving it.

Establishing a Balance in The Global Company

Klaus H. Dunst

Vice President, Corporate Development
Siemens Corporation

In corporate development at Siemens U.S., we balance U.S. regional interests with those of headquarters in Munich. Siemens operates globally in the electrical and electronic market and has about $43 billion in sales, 75 percent of which are in Europe. We need to improve our competitive position in the United States and Japan and to expand in regions such as the Pacific Rim and North America. Thus, our worldwide strategy incorporates strategies for specific countries.

Overall Organization

The central executive committee controls major resource allocations but our organization is decentralized. We have 16 groups with worldwide responsibility for products ranging from semiconductors to entire electrical generating plants. With worldwide responsibility for product development, production, sales and marketing, each group consists of businesses organized around specific markets. Most of the product groups are represented in 1 of the 8 major U.S. operating companies. Each U.S. operating company has a board of directors that includes both group and corporate management. The board approves investment proposals which are then approved at the corporate level. Any issues and conflicts among the groups are usually resolved in the U.S. company boards—in extraordinary cases, they are brought to the attention of the central executive committee.

Building on Strength in the United States

As the United States represents 26 percent of the world market, our strategy calls for expanding here. Siemens U.S. sales growth in the last five years was 17 percent a year, about 7 percentage points by acquisition and 10 percentage points through internal growth. U.S. sales grew from 3 percent of Siemens' worldwide revenue in the early 1980s to about 10 percent in the late '80s. Our goal for this decade is to achieve about 20 percent in the United States.

U.S. market size, specific customer demands, and the availability of technical skills prompted our expansion. Close to two-thirds of our U.S. business is now in the medical, energy and automation businesses. While our share of the overall U.S. market is only 1 percent, we are among the top three suppliers in certain segments. We now have 60 manufacturing locations here. Significant R&D investments—about $400 million in 1989 to 1990—support manufacturing, marketing and sales efforts.

Balancing Regional and Central Responsibility

At Siemens, global strategy formulation does not mean centralized control. Developing corporate strategy includes the active involvement of senior managers of our major regional companies. Siemens Corporation in the United States acts as a management holding company supporting the group's worldwide strategies while also representing Siemens' overall U.S. interests.

How we balance central and regional responsibilities for value-adding activities—product development, manufacturing, selling and service—depends on the type of business. Some businesses have the entire value chain within their home markets, from which they may also export. Others are based in a certain region but draw on value-adding activities from elsewhere. The remaining businesses encompass the entire value chain regionally and have some worldwide responsibilities.

Siemens U.S. is one of these businesses. For example, as a worldwide competence center for selected medical equipment, Siemens is a U.S.-based business exporting to Europe and to other regions.

Achieving Competitive Advantage Globally

Building competitive edge is the essence of any global strategy. One can gain competitive advantage by concentrating and/or by coordinating value-adding activities. Concentrating value-adding activities can bring substantial cost advantages from economies of scale. The manufacture of personal computers or integrated circuits is an example. Yet concentration may not be necessary and can be counterproductive. New forms of flexible automation reduce the significance of volume as a cost driver. And some customers prefer to pay a premium for tailored products rather than take cheaper standard products. Smaller production sites closer to customers meet such needs and can provide more timely responses.

Increasingly, achieving global competitive advantage will call for the coordination of value-adding activities. Effective coordination requires clearly defined regional responsibilities. Thus, one region's responsibilities might include marketing and sales, while product development and production are the responsibility of another region—or managed centrally. This complexity makes effective communication systems essential. Also essential are suitable personnel policies. Employees at corporate headquarters and at regional units must have shared goals and values. The result is not only coordination but a functioning balance between central and regional interests.

Resourceful Strategy Development Requires Self-Reliance

Donald A. Laidlaw

IBM Director, Executive Resources and Development
IBM Corporation

Human resources activities have often been perceived as tactical, as part of implementation. In the 1990s, there is a genuine need and an opportunity to influence the strategies themselves.

Over the next decade demand for critical skills will exceed the supply. Declining birth rates in industrial countries mean a declining entry-level labor pool. Our educational system is not producing the skilled people we need. Escalating use of technology calls for skills that may be in short supply worldwide. Inside companies, skills are often unbalanced as a result of restructuring efforts. As much as 85 percent of the work force growth will come from women, U.S.-born minorities, and immigrants. It's little wonder that top managements' attention to human resources is growing.

Competitive position depends on providing the best quality products and services at the best price in the shortest time. When employees don't have the right skills at the right time, the company will not be the lowest cost producer, it will not have the highest quality, nor will it be first in the marketplace. Increasingly, the human resources executive is included in top strategy sessions. Occasionally, a top business leader's background even includes human resource experience.

Effective human resources executives contribute to a company's strategic advantage. There is no one best way to do so but I have some recommendations. First, they should develop a broader perspective and understand the business' products, strengths and weaknesses, competition, and financial outlook.

My second recommendation is to strengthen human resources planning. This must include interpreting information from all sources and projecting the impact of demographics, economic trends, changing value systems, and social issues.

Finally, I recommend that human resources people—at all levels—become more proactive. For example, many companies are downsizing or restructuring. Human resources professionals should already have a program ready with supporting cost-benefit analysis.

Human Resources' Greatest Contributions

There are several areas where human resources can help fill the company's need to attract, retain and develop a quality work force:

Employment policies. Work arrangements (for example, flexible schedules, job sharing and work-at-home) should reflect the diverse needs of your work force.

Leave policies. These include both personal leave and educational leave for the sake of the employee and the business.

Employee services, such as child care, elder care referral, and employee assistance and wellness programs.

Benefits eligibility to recognize changing lifestyles.

Work force education. This is one I would emphasize. It covers basic skills, such as language and math, soft skills in communication, teamwork and networking, and technical skills upgrades.

Reward systems. These must tie in with company expectations of quality, innovation, risk, and knowledge while recognizing employees' responsiveness, participation and contributions.

These days, there are many significant ways that the human resource function can contribute to business strategies. Having top management's attention is a help. But it's up to the human resources people themselves to take the initiative.

Human Resources Actions to Support Strategy Implementation

John R. Loya
Vice President, Human Resources
Northwestern Memorial Hospital

Disenchantment with strategic planning is, I believe, largely the result of failures in implementation. A common cause of implementation problems is the conflict between the strategies and the management systems, especially the human resources system.

An academic medical center, Northwestern Memorial Hospital provides patient care, education and research. We treat about 26,000 inpatients annually and several times that number of outpatients, generating about $400 million in revenues and employing more than 4,500 people. Our challenges are similar to other organizations', especially those affected by deregulation: Competition is great and cost pressures are intense.

Removing Implementation Barriers

Our vision is to be the dominant health care provider in Chicago and a leading academic medical center nationwide. When formulating our strategies, we defined specific human resource issues, but when trying to translate strategy into operating plans, we identified major barriers to implementation. These are:

- high turnover among lower-level managers most of whom work part-time and lack management training;

- too many layers of management with inconsistent roles and bureaucratic policies;

- conflicting priorities, uncoordinated efforts, low accountability and a hospital-wide lack of customer orientation; and

- inadequate line manager support from staff functions—information services, finance and human resources.

The human resources division is working to remove these barriers. Two major initiatives are:

1. *Focus the organization on its primary mission.* This involves reducing the number of management layers and the number of managers; defining full-time manager jobs and streamlining management processes; increasing resources for caregiving; and focusing all departments on providing top quality care.

2. *Enable our managers to be more self-reliant and our employees to deliver the best care possible.* This requires reorganizing the human resources division to support client services teams, and modifying all major human resources systems, including the reward system.

Successful efforts of this kind pave the way for smooth and effective strategy implementation.

Human Resources:
The Ultimate Advantage

David L. Hertz
President
Quality Educational Development, Inc.

These days, human resource strategy is a key ingredient in creating sustained competitive advantage. That people are the most valuable resource is now well-accepted. Balancing the needs of the business with the needs of its employees is a critical responsibility that line and human resources executives share. Business needs a skilled, productive and innovative work force; employees, on the other hand, seek self-fulfillment—and consider their skills "portable." Companies must therefore strive to compensate for a deficient educational system, resolve work-family conflicts, and win employees' allegiance.

Making Employees Feel Needed

For business vitality, strategic planning must enhance individuals' contributions. A long-term plan should:

- develop broadly experienced, strategically oriented, entrepreneurial managers. This requires making jobs more meaningful by defining them in terms of end results, not tasks.

- flatten the organization to create broader opportunities for managers and workers alike. Wider spans of control discourage managers' over-attention to detail and encourage workers' involvement and contribution.

- encourage disciplined planning to develop mutually acceptable performance criteria. This clarifies expectations on both sides and focuses efforts on business objectives.

- design reward systems to recognize employees' contribution to business success. Balancing individual versus team efforts, long-range versus short-term results, and results versus activities are key considerations in designing these reward systems.

Integrating human resource activities with strategy calls for collaboration between line and human resources executives at corporate and business unit levels. Human resource activities need to address real, specific business issues to strengthen the company's ability to compete.

Human Resources Stra[tegy]
Must Support Busines[s Strategy]

Russell W. Boekenheide
Senior Vice President
Human Resources and Administration
Union Camp Corporation

Union Camp makes paper, packaging, chem[icals]
and building products. Manufacturing the[se]
products is capital intensive. For example[, to]
keep production equipment up to date, we spent m[ore]
than $2.3 billion over the past five years. This doe[s not]
mean equipment is more important than people. W[e typ-]
ically spend $25 million a year training people to [use]
that equipment. Moreover, since our competitors [also]
have access to the same equipment, it's the way o[ur peo-]
ple use it that gives us a competitive edge.

Key to a Human Resources-Business Strateg[y] Partnership

There are two key elements to a successful human re-
sources-business strategy partnership. These are the
position of human resources in the organizational structure and the competency and orientation of the human
resources staff.

Human resources (HR) must be positioned where it
can influence business planning. This is more an issue
of attitude and culture than of organizational level. HR
at Union Camp is considered an essential element of
our business and our HR professionals have the access,
power and autonomy they need to get things done. For
example, being on our capital expenditure committee,
I'm involved in all our major projects, mergers and
acquisitions. Human resources is also a full participant
in formal long-range planning meaning that the plans
incorporate the HR issues key to achieving the corporation's strategic goals. Last year, for example, we identified issues and action plans to deal with emerging
demographic trends, such as growth in the number
of women and minorities and shortfall of technically
qualified entrants.

[...a]t the operating
[...d]evelops a man-
[...k]ind of people
[...deve]lopment of high-
[...]s are presented to
[...bo]ard of directors.
[...]tional positioning
[...] and orientation
[...profess]ional competence
[...] people. They
[...contrib]ute to the busi-
[...] who are creative
and visionary but also action-oriented and capable of developing practical solutions. We have developed this
kind of person who now sits at the right hand of operating managers at all levels, from corporate offices to the
plant level. Our HR people know what's going on and
their advice is solicited and taken seriously. In fact, operating managers are constantly recruiting these people
for line jobs. Two division vice presidents, one division
manager, and three plant managers all started their ca-
reers in human resources.

Human Resources and Capital Investments

Like other companies, we custom design our new facilities using the best technology and equipment
available. But we also custom design the human resources aspects of a new operation. For example, before
the first design for a state-of-the-art paper mill was put
to paper we had developed and executed a state-of-the-
art human resources plan. We built a new work force
from scratch, ignoring all preconceptions about how a
paper mill should be staffed; we hired all inexperienced